Creative Parent Communication

Graphic Arts for Teachers' Notes

Pamela Tuchscherer

Pinnaroo Publishing

The author gratefully acknowledges the permission granted from the National Association for the Advancement of Humane Education to reproduce animal clip art from **The Miniature Menagerie—A Portfolio of Humane Education Clip Art**.

Copyright ©1986 by Pinnaroo Publishing
First Edition 1986

All rights reserved. The pages of this book may be copied only for internal or personal use to share with parents and teachers. No part of this work covered by the copyright hereon may be reproduced in any form for profit making means or resale.

ISBN: 0-939705-00-1

Design and Production: Tyson Tuchscherer

Pinnaroo Publishing
P.O. Box 7525
Bend, Oregon 97708

Printed in the United States of America

Introduction

Parents are busy people, yet they want and need to know what goes on at school. They look forward to learning about their child's classroom experiences and appreciate receiving news of classroom schedules and procedures. **Creative Parent Communication** is designed to assist you in conveying this information to parents in a positive and creative way.

In order for notes or letters to be effective, they first have to be noticed and secondly, read. The appearance of your communique conveys more than the stated message—if it is displayed attractively, it will show parents that you felt they were worth your extra time and attention.

Creative Parent Communication contains letter shells for common situations such as invitations to the classroom, rainy-day procedures and daily schedule changes as well as formats for messages dealing with specific areas of the curriculum such as: science, nutrition, art, safety, health, classroom activities, reading, and social development.

Need to send a memo—"I can't find it anywhere!"? A letter shell thoughtfully transmitting this message is included. There are also letter shells for special messages to individual parents describing positive accomplishments and for interstaff notices. At the end of the book, you will find a selection of extra clip art, dashed lines and headings that can be used to adapt the letter shells to your needs or create your own "noticeable notes."

In addition to clarifying classroom activities and procedures, other suggestions for parent communication are:

1) Describe related activities parents can do at home with their child. For example, give a brief description of a cooking experience and place one of the class's favorite recipes on the bottom of the nutrition shell.

2) Periodically write a letter explaining things of interest to children outside the classroom—community activities, comments on educational toys, etc.

3) When sending home examples of students work, add a letter explaining its purpose. This allows parents to better understand their child's learning experience.

4) Provide parent notes summarizing specific activities and problems the class has faced. By leaving space for a personal note about each child and a space for parent comments, open communication will be encouraged.

5) Planning on conferences? Why not send a reminder sheet home to parents a week ahead asking them to jot down any questions or concerns they might have.

6) For parents who receive the answer, "I don't know" to their question, "What did you do at school today?", a note with "quizillating questions" may be the answer. Quizillating questions are questions you can provide parents which relate directly to activities and materials covered during the day or week. For example: If you have been studying shapes, suggest that the parent ask a related question such as: "Can you find any rectangles in the kitchen?"

7. Share information dealing with the education of the whole child, at home as well as at school. One such topic is the effect of television on children and ways to encourage parents to monitor their children's viewing.

To assist parents in using television to help, not harm their children, Dr. Bernadette Angle, of Youngstown State University, has written a list of suggestions. This popular copy item for teachers has been included for your use. See the page titled, **9 Ways to Use TV to Help, Not Harm, Your Child**.

Creative Parent Communications is designed for you. There are unlimited possibilities to the ways you can use the letter shells. Have fun, be creative with your parent notes and you'll find that well-informed parents will show more interest and readily respond to your "noticeable notes".

Making Copies

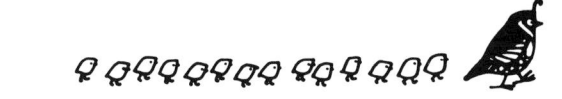

Photocopy or Quick Print

For best reproduction of the letter shells, photocopy or quick print them. If you are planning to make more than 100 copies, often quick printing is less expensive. Remove desired letter shell from book by carefully tearing along perforated edge, then use one of the following two ways to prepare your letter:

1) Simply cut a piece of clean white paper so that it will fit in the space provided without covering the clip art or border lines.

—Write or type your note with black ink. Keep in mind the final product and adjust your spacing so that you can obtain the "look" you want.

—Attach the note with rubber cement or clear cellophane tape (rolled and attached underneath), so that you can remove it easily.

Remember: If you have your letter quick printed, be sure to check that all the pieces are securely attached and the original is clean. You can use white out (available at stationary stores) to cover any unwanted marks.

2) Make a good, dark photocopy of the letter shell (be sure to include any additional clip art you want).

—Write your note with black ink on this photocopied sheet.

—Then, using this photocopy as an original, print the number of copies you need.

Remember: While using the photocopy machine you may want to run off extra copies of letter shells to have on hand for individual notes.

Making a Master

If you plan to make ink-based masters from the letter shells, you will need to use a Thermofax machine (or facsimile). This machine, found in many schools and offices, can create an ink-based master from your original which you can use on a duplicating machine. There are two ways to prepare your letter shell to be used to make the master:

1) Place the letter shell into the master unit and remove the tissue sheet. Place the master unit into the plastic holder and feed it into the machine. Then, write your note on the master (with shell design on it).

2) Place the letter shell, with your note attached, into the master unit. Remove the tissue sheet and place the master unit (containing your letter) into the plastic holder and feed it into the machine.

Once you have torn off the ink-based master, you can use it on your duplicating machine to run the number of copies you need.

Remember: After your copies have been made don't forget to retain your original letter shell and place it back in the book for safe keeping. The cleaner the original is kept, the nicer your following letters will be.

Keep the masters of all your notes and any additional clip art used in an envelope and store them with your book. This will allow you to refer to notes you have written and to have materials ready for the next time you need them.

The animal clip art in **Creative Parent Communication** was used by permission of the National Association for the Advancement of Humane Education (NAAHE) from their portfolio **The Miniature Menagerie—A Portfolio of Humane Education Clip Art**.

The Miniature Menagerie contains clip art comprised of animal illustrations by various artists that is ideal for use on handouts, newsletters and announcements. Other uses for the clip art is to make classroom games or puzzles, make bookmarkers or add interest to bulletin boards. Contents include ten 17"x11" sheets and helpful how-to instructions on the use of clip art.

Miniature Menagerie (HE 1028) is available for $4. To order, send remittance and publication name and number to:

NAAHE
Box 362
East Haddam, CT 06423

Communication is the key.

Come Join Us

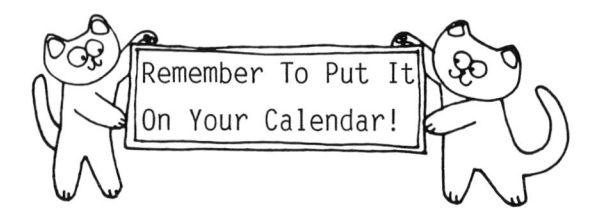

Remember To Put It On Your Calendar!

"...children relish that special moment when a person gives them time and attention."

Charles A. Smith

You're Invited

IT'LL BE FUN!

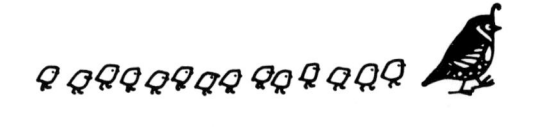

We're Going A Field

"Look at everything as though you have never seen it before."   Paul Valery

"It is the supreme art of the teacher to awaken joy in creative expression and knowledge."

Albert Einstein

Library News

"A teacher has to be a prophet who can look
into the future and see the world of tomorrow
into which the children of today must fit."

Anonymous

Schedule Change

Our Day

Will Be

Shorter

"From the very beginning of his education the child should experience the joy of discovery."   — Alfred North Whitehead

YOU'D BE PROUD!

"Nothing ever becomes real till it is experienced." John Keats

**This is a definition a child once gave of 'Creative Art':
"I think and then I draw a line around my think."**

Emily Carr

Health

It's That Time Of Year

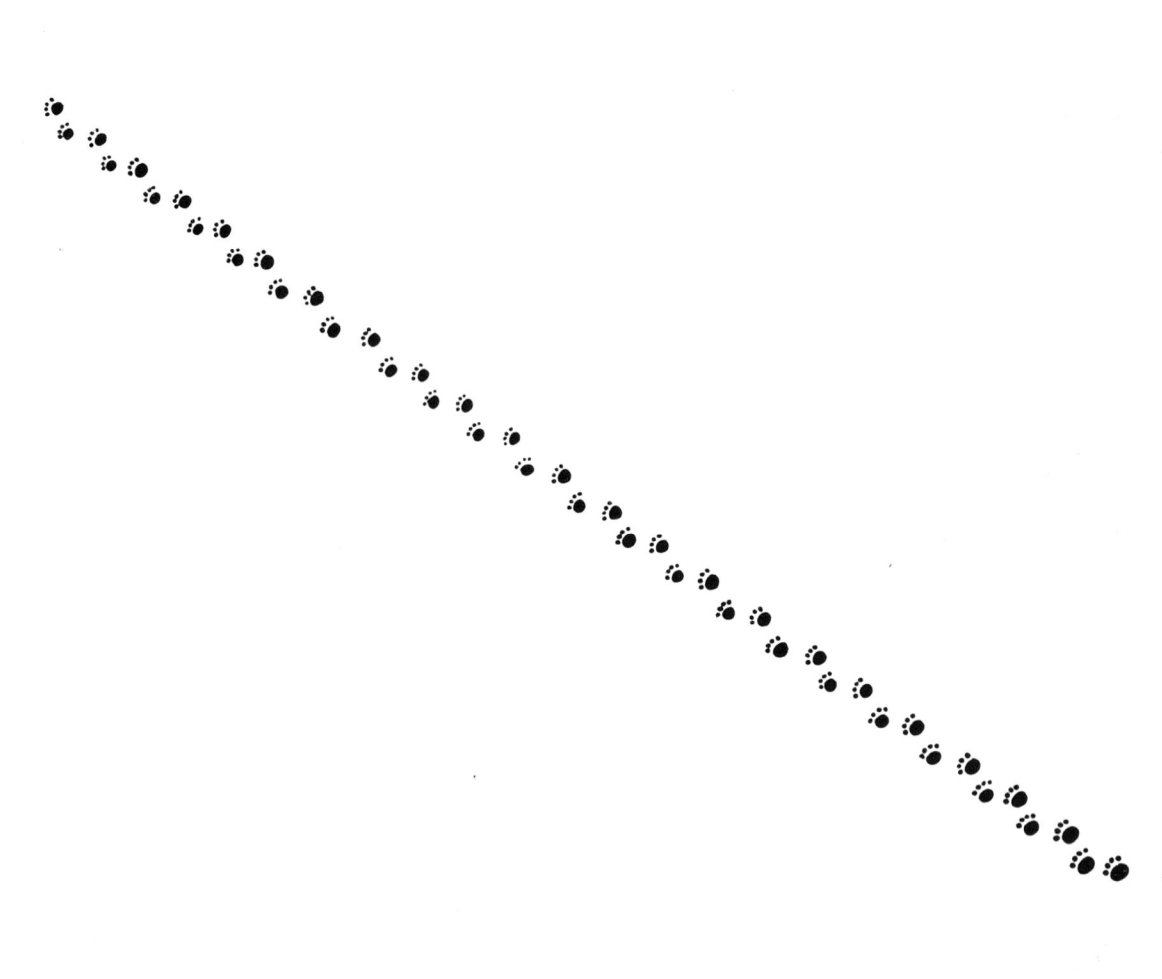

Safety

Swimming Lesson

Permission Slip

"I can't find it anywhere!"

Please return promptly

I know you have to cope with

and

not to mention a

once in a while,

but please take time to:

Communication

One of the most important aspects of school is peer interaction and the relationships that develop.

"Children have real understanding only of that
which they invent themselves, and each time that
we try to teach them something too quickly, we
keep them from re-inventing it themselves."

Jean Piaget

"...the more interests a child has at least a chance to acquire, the more chance he will have to hit upon some interests that are suited to his particular gifts."

Arthur T. Jersild

"Our children need to be treated as human beings—exquisite, complex and elegant in their diversity."

Lloyd Dennis

"Play...is a way of learning by trial and error to
cope with the actual world."

Lawrence Frank

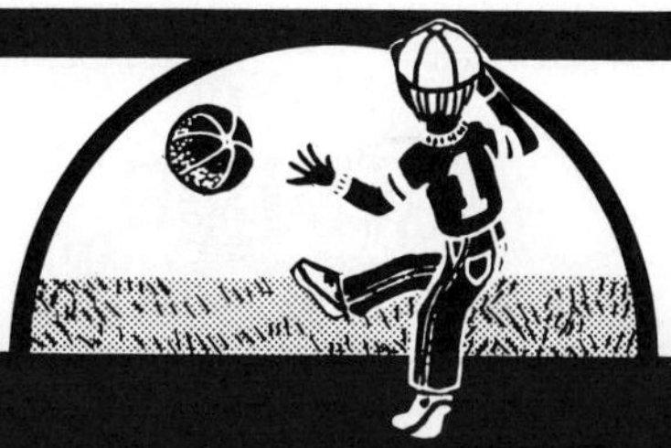

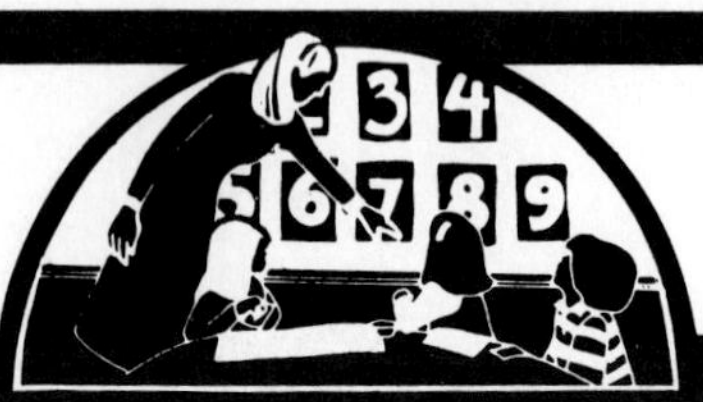
3 4
6 7 8 9

For Your Information:

9 Ways to Use TV to Help, Not Harm, Your Child

1 **Don't use TV as a babysitter.** It may seem easier to place children in front of the television regardless of the quality of programming when you are busy around the house, but remember, children build strong family ties from their participation in household chores and shopping. Include them in these activities.

2 **Carefully select the shows your family watches.** Be the parent and insist that certain shows are off limits.

3 **Set aside a time for "family shows," programs you watch together.** When parents and children express views about the program's content and exchange ideas, family members gain insights about the program and each other.

4 **Include children in family decisions about what you will watch together.** This shows children their ideas are respected and can set the stage for family meetings to discuss other family projects.

5 **Be a model for your child.** Choose carefully the programs you watch.

6 **Don't use TV as a reward or punishment.** As such, it can become a crutch which places too much value on the medium. Instead, try to think of something more directly tied to the child's behavior.

7 **Join with other parents in your community to press for more and better programs for children and families.** Organized viewers do make a difference. You may also want to contact the national advocacy group Action for Children's Television, 46 Austin St., Newtonville, MA 02160.

8 **Use activities like the following to enhance the learning value of the TV shows you watch as a family:**

- Ask your child to exercise his/her imagination and think of another title for the program or series you are watching.

- Read newspaper articles together describing the show before watching it. Have your child write a description or narration of the program after viewing it.

- During a commercial break ask your child to predict what will happen next.

- Turn off the volume but leave the picture on. Ask your child to guess what is happening by watching the action without the sound.

- Have your child draw a picture describing his feelings about a show. Discuss the picture together.

- Ask your child to time the commercials during a show then add them together.

9 **Be as selective with your child's TV diet as you are with what he or she eats.** Just as we are what we eat, to some extent; so too we are what we watch!

By Bernadette Angle, Ph.D., Associate Professor at Youngstown State University, Special Education Department.

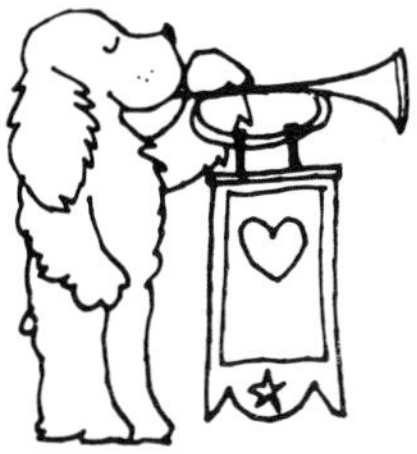
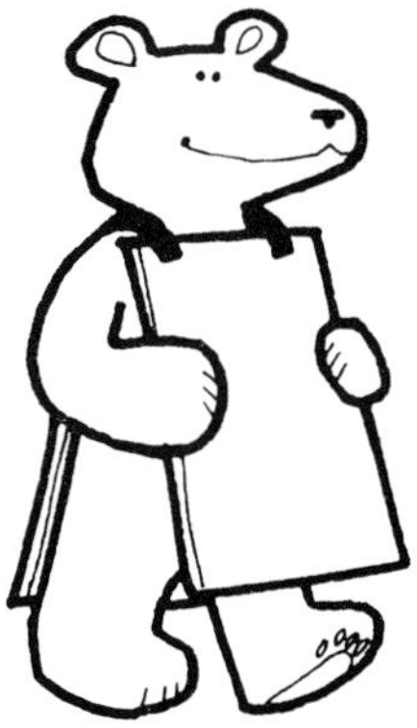
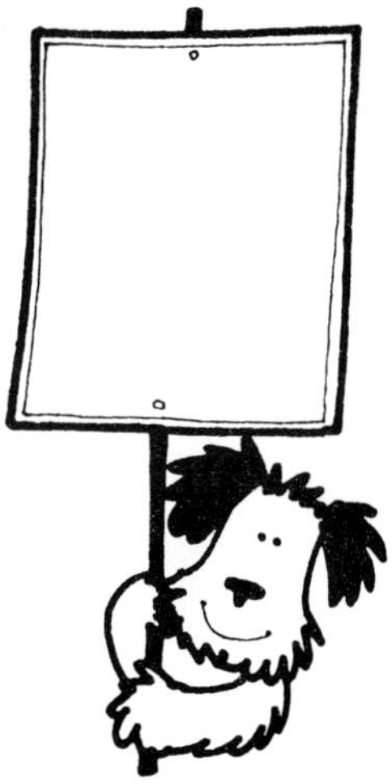
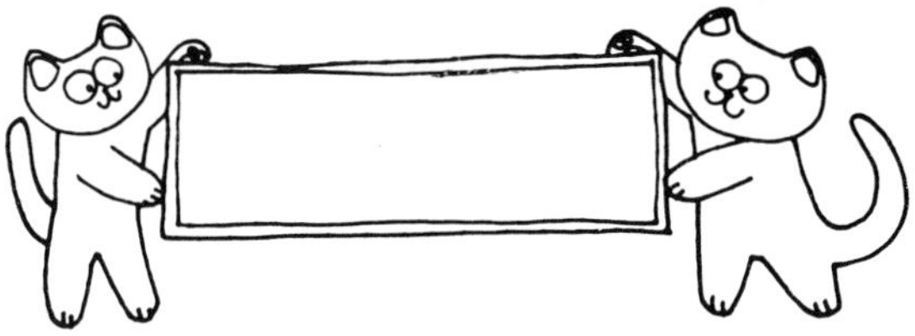
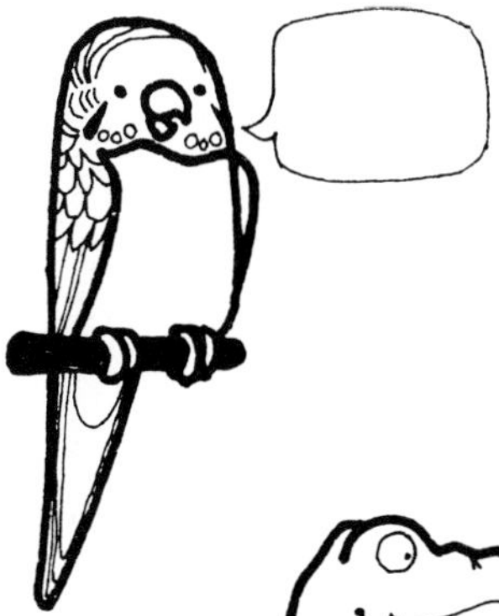
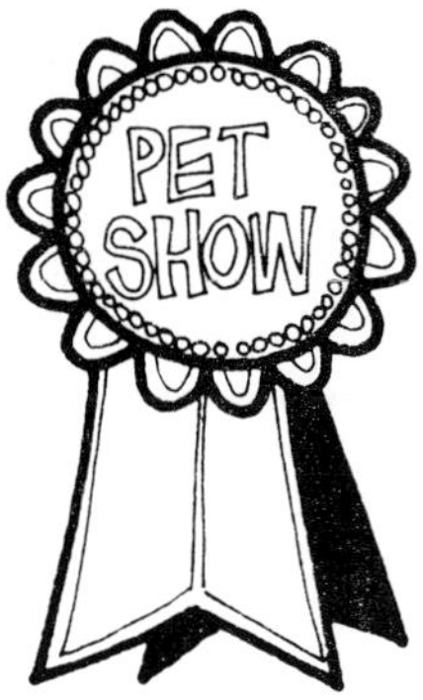
PET SHOW
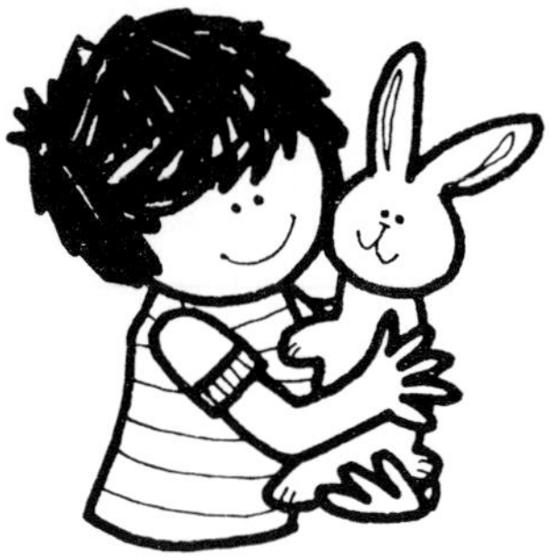
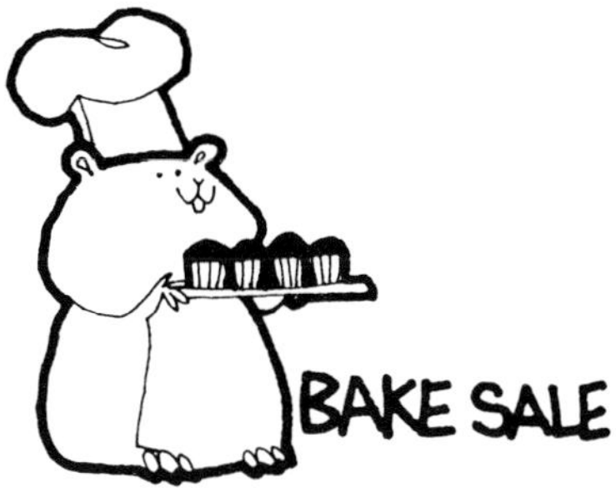
BAKE SALE
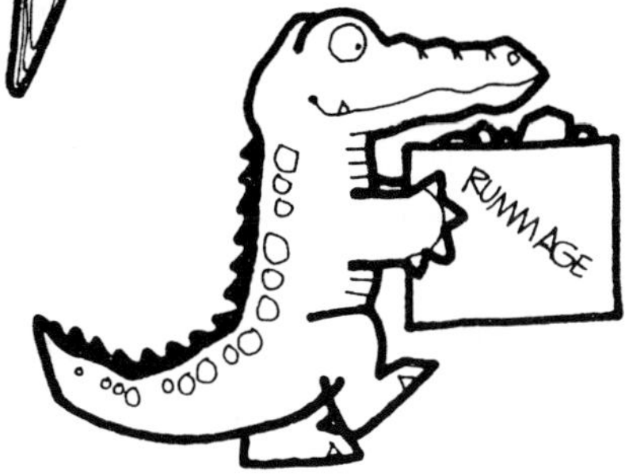
RUMMAGE
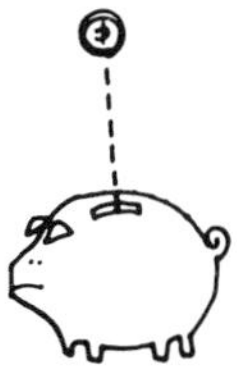
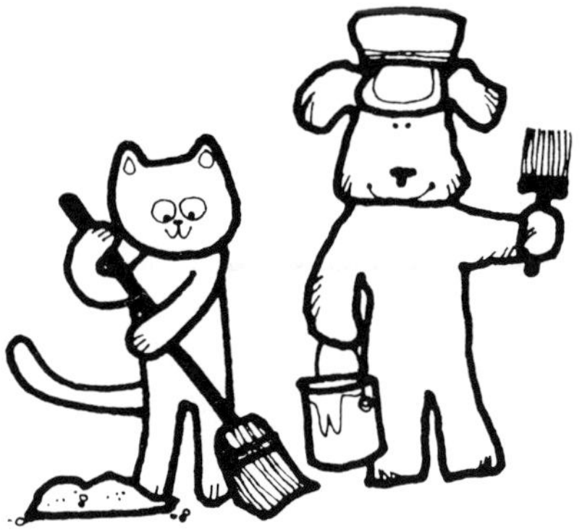
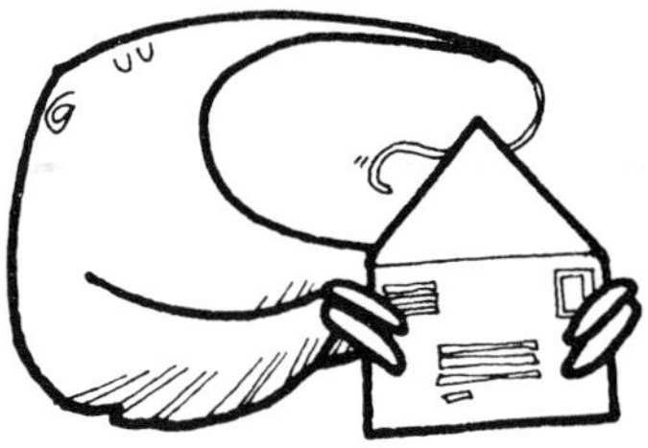
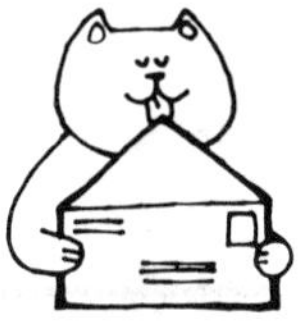
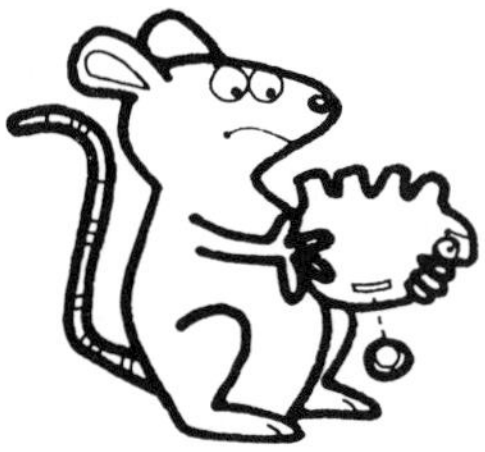
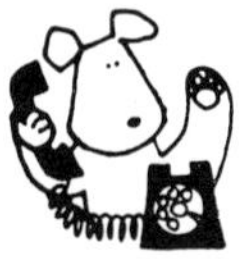
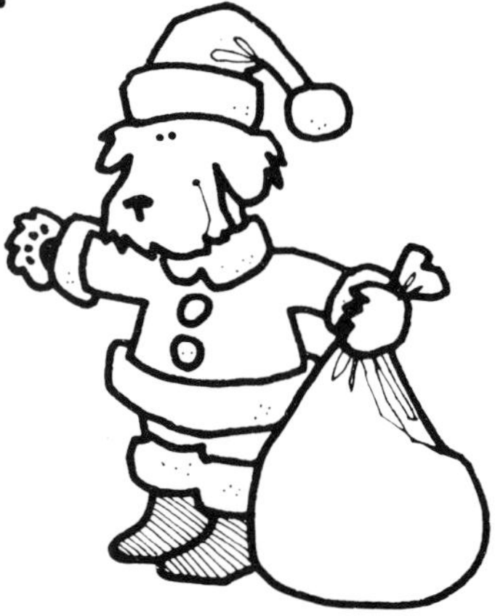

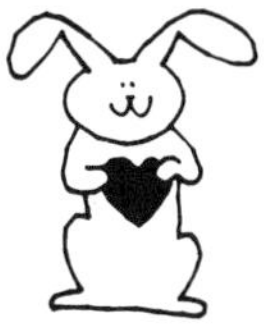
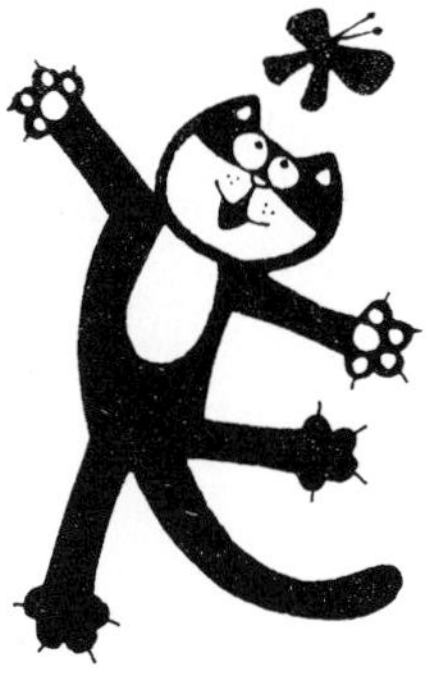

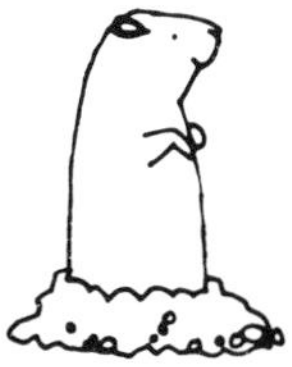
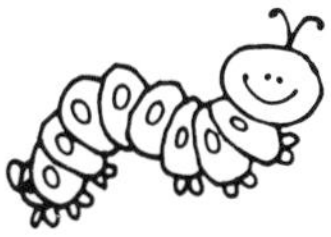
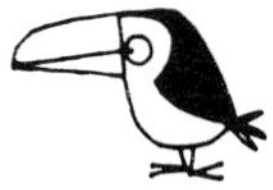
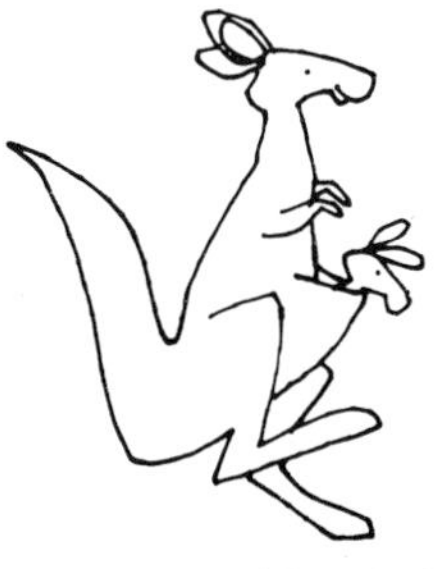

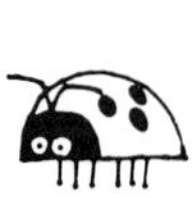
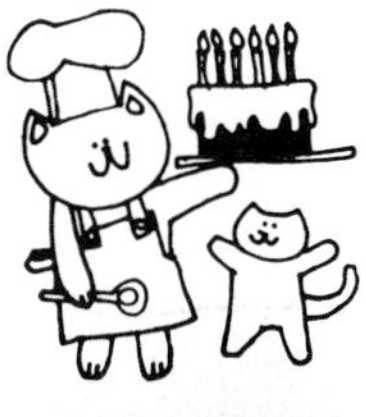
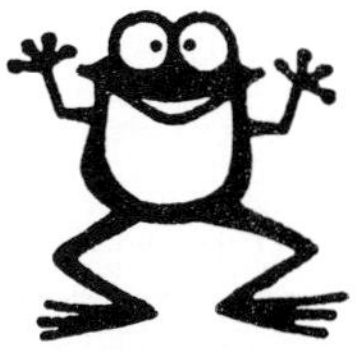
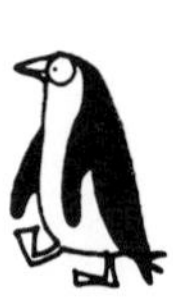
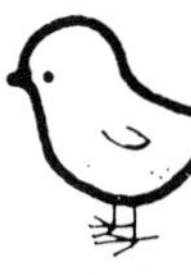

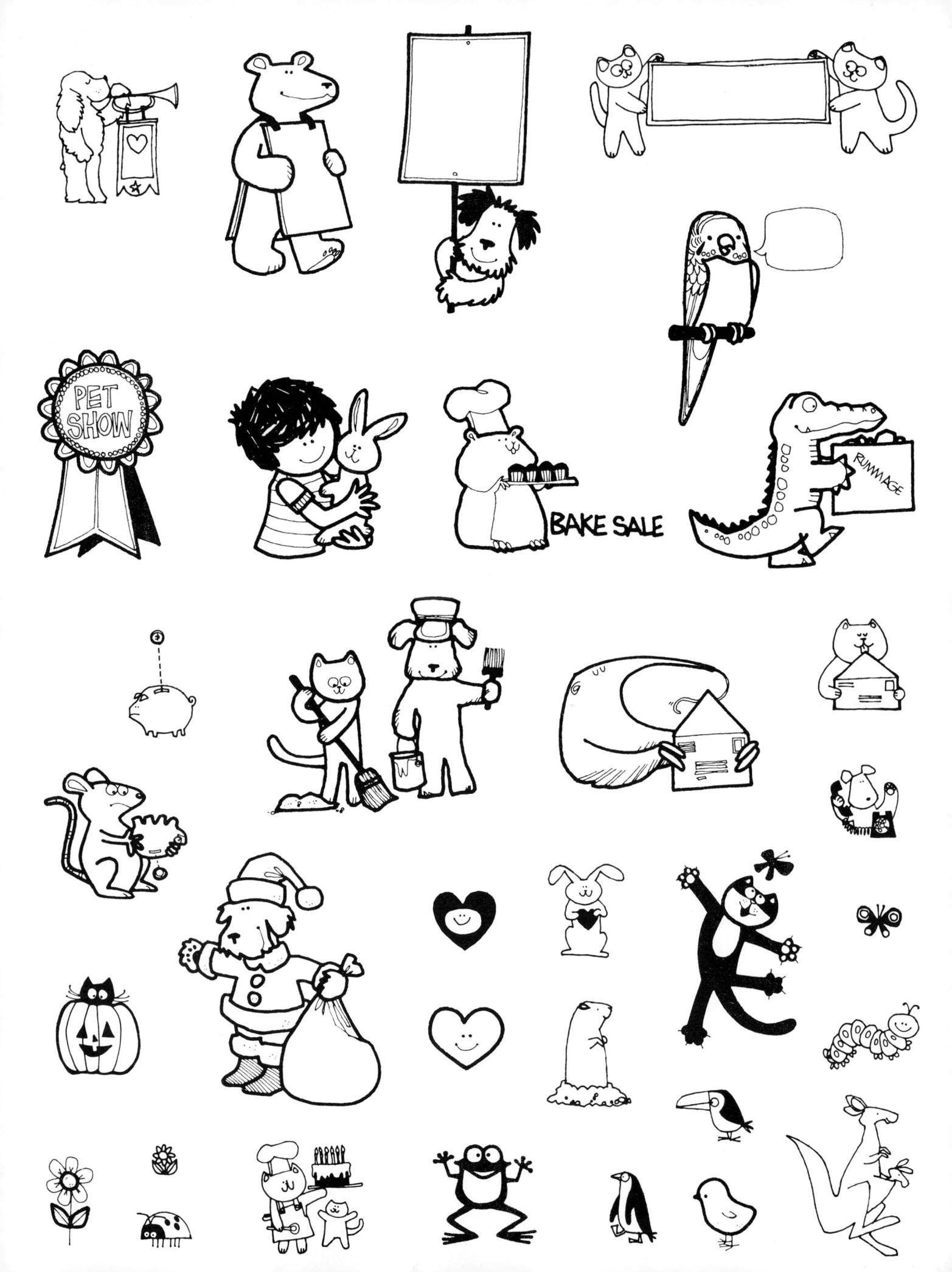

Y

C

S

S

G

Y

Y

W

P

Plea
Don

If y

"F
mos

Additional Copies

Use this form to order additional copies of **Creative Parent Communication**, or other related publications.

Creative Parent Communication /$7.97/

Where's the best place to get the information you need to enhance the learning process?

Early Educator's Tool Box,

a single source reference gives you the answer. This guide to Early Childhood programs and materials supplies not only comprehensive descriptions of resources, but gives insight into how teachers use many of them in their classroom.

- Up-to-date guide to over 100 resources covering an array of topics.
    - —Nutrition   —Science   —Volunteers
    - —Health   —Special Needs   —Parent Communication
    - —Safety   —Multicultural   —Administration
    - —Art   —Classroom Activities

- Table of Contents and Index for easy reference

- Illustrated and easy to read

- 160 pages / 8½" x 11" / Soft Cover / $12.95

- Tools to help you build your classroom resources and supplement your curriculum—all within your budget.

Educators can you afford the time and cost of attending workshops each month?

If not, try **Preschool Perspectives**, the newsletter for educators of young children. Get stimulating new ideas each month on Early Childhood Education — new resources, teaching strategies, child development, management and much more.

Preschool Perspectives can keep you up-to-date on new developments in Early Childhood Education. Yet, its concise, non-clinical articles will allow you to keep informed despite your busy schedule.

Gold Award winner "for overall excellence" — 13th Annual Newsletter Award Competition, Washington, D.C., June 1985

Send for your free sample Today!

☐ **Creative Parent Communication** .... $ 7.95

☐ **Early Educators Tool Box** $12.95

(Please add $2 for postage and handling for one book, 50¢ for each additional book)..................... _____

Total Enclosed .... _____

☐ **Preschool Perspectives** .... Free Sample

Name _____

Address _____

City _____ State _____ Zip _____

Mail to: **Pinnaroo Publishing**
           P.O. Box 7525
           Bend, OR 97708